My Hijab and me

MAYMUUNA YUS

Published by Abāyo House
Visit our website at www.abayohouse.com
ISBN: 978-1-7771151-8-0

My hijab & me is dedicated to all my sisters in faith.

My Hijab
and me

Is a beautiful
story you see

My Hijab is a protection

That God
ordained for me

My Hijab is like a cloak

Much cooler
than any
cape

My mom wears the hijab

My sisters
wear it

The lady accross
the street

and my teacher
at school!

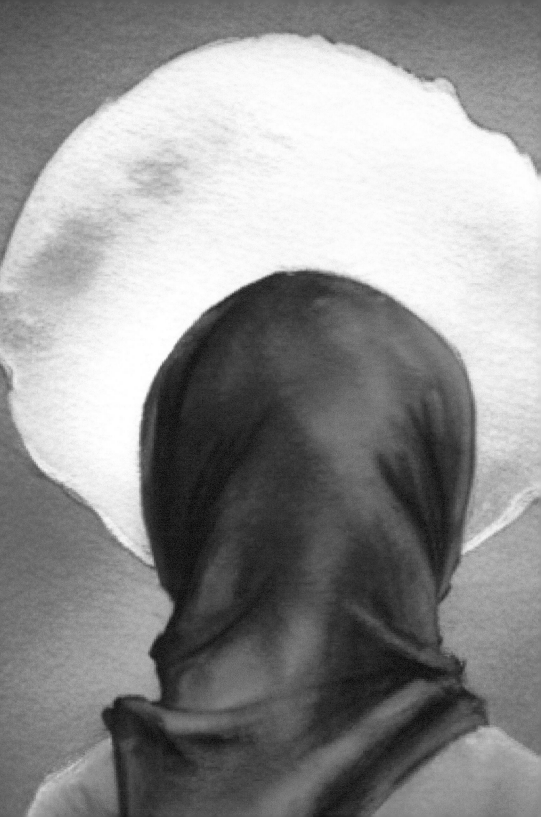

There are many things I love about the hijab

I can wear it
in so many
colours

Even my
favourite
colour
PINK

My Hijab
and me

Is a
beautiful
story you
see

Hijab tells people of my faith

so I wear my
islam with
delight

and when
people ask
me with
disdain

on why wear
a cloth so
mundane

I
simply
tell
them

My Hijab and me

Is
MY
story
you
see

It is a
promise
between
God and me

What does Hijab mean to you?

colour your favourite hijab

Maymuuna Yusuf

Maymuuna is one of the founding members of
Abāyo House. She is an educator, writer, editor
and publisher. She has a bachelor's degree in
Education from the University of Alberta, Canada.
Maymuuna is passionate about education and
aims to contribute meaningful practices to her
teaching. Her goal is to develop resources where
every student feels seen in the classroom through
books. She wants to live in a literary world where
every child has the experience of reading inspiring
and engaging stories that represent them.
Maymuuna believes love for writing starts in the
classroom. As students learn the foundations of
writing, she is also determined to help them
develop ownership and pride over their own
stories. After all, there are stories swimming in each
of us that are waiting to be shared.

 @abayohouse

Milton Keynes UK
Ingram Content Group UK Ltd.
UKHW050316130224
437742UK00002B/50